The Field and The Knower

"There is suffering."

Copyright © 2024 iC7Zi.
All rights reserved.
Published by iC7Zi
ISBN 9798343951134

Table of Contents

Suffering and Shadows	4
• There is suffering	
• Uniting the Psyche	
The Anchor	14
• Understanding the Field and the Knower	
• Mastering the Modifications of the Field	
• Dissolving Ego and False Identity	
• Cultivating Non-Attachment and Equanimity	
• Seeking Knowledge of the Self	
• Surrender and Devotion	
• Seeing the Unity in All Beings	
The Hermetic Path	36
• The Principle of Mentalism	
• The Principle of Correspondence	
• The Principle of Vibration	
• The Principle of Polarity	
• The Principle of Rhythm	
• The Principle of Cause and Effect	
• The Principle of Gender	
• The 21 Shadows	
In Surrender, We Awaken	49
• Cycle of Seeking	
• The Dance of Unity: A Poem	
• Harnessing Chaos	
• Rise and Rewrite the Story: A Poem	

Twelve Seconds Too Soon: A Story • Dance with Life • Hands of the Unseen: A Poem	60
Transmuting Shadows: "I Am" affirmations • Pride into Humility • Fear into Courage • Anger into Forgiveness • Jealousy into Contentment • Shame into Self-Worth • Guilt into Self-Forgiveness • Control into Surrender • Greed into Generosity • Arrogance into Open-Mindedness • Self-doubt into Confidence • Addiction into Self-Mastery • Judgment into Compassion • Victimhood into Empowerment • Laziness into Motivation • Narcissism into Empathy • Self-sabotage into Self-Commitment • Perfectionism into Self-Acceptance • Resentment into Release • Apathy into Passion • Over-identification into Soul Alignment • Intolerance into Unity	67
Cosmic Comedy: A Poem	114

Suffering and Shadows

Suffering is inevitable. This is not a pessimistic view but a reality observed by every major spiritual tradition, especially Buddhism. The Buddha's first noble truth declares,

> "There is suffering."

From birth to death, through sickness, aging, loss, and death, suffering weaves its way into every facet of existence. Physical suffering is one thing, but mental suffering—anxiety, despair, fear, loneliness—torments the modern person in ways far more subtle and pervasive.

As the Buddha stated,

> "Attachment is the root of suffering."

The constant identification with thoughts, emotions, and desires perpetuates the mental anguish that many try to avoid or suppress. Yet, no amount of material wealth, relationships, or fleeting pleasure can shield anyone from this suffering.

The mind, with its endless cycles of craving and aversion, guarantees it. The shadow is growing—whether through personal loss, global crises, or the internal battles of the mind, suffering is at our doorstep.

However, we are not powerless. Non-attachment is the key. But non-attachment is not about being numb; it is about anchoring yourself so deeply within that the external storm cannot shake your inner core.

Meditation and self-reflection become the foundation of this inner strength. As the Buddha taught,

> "Peace comes from within. Do not seek it without."

But to cultivate this inner peace, you must practice it rigorously.

Building a strong anchor point in meditation is essential to minimize suffering. This anchor is what prevents the mind from being swept away by the inevitable hardships of life.

Non-attachment requires consistency, not just intellectual understanding.

It is a practice of letting go, not just of material things, but of identification with the ego self. The *Bhagavad Gita* states:

> "When a man gives up all desires that enter his mind and when he is satisfied within himself by himself, then he is said to be steady in wisdom."

Prepare yourself. Suffering will come, but through a steady practice of non-attachment and meditation, you can develop the resilience to endure it. "Pain is certain, suffering is optional," said the Buddha.

The shadow of suffering will always be present, but you are not defenseless. Strengthen your anchor.

We must first accept that we are bound by the ego. The mind, though often revered as our greatest asset, can also be our greatest obstacle. It isn't as flawless as we might think.

There is no shame in acknowledging this. In fact, true strength lies in openly confronting the parts of ourselves we prefer to hide —the shadow aspects that shape much of our suffering.

The shadow, in all its forms, is something we all carry within us. Whether it's unprocessed emotions, unresolved trauma, or traits we reject in ourselves, the shadow is a powerful force. Denying it only strengthens its hold. As Carl Jung famously said,

> "Until you make the unconscious conscious, it will direct your life and you will call it fate."

It's not about pretending the shadow doesn't exist or feeling ashamed of it. It's about bringing it to light through awareness. The moment you acknowledge your shadow is the moment transformation can begin.

We should make it a habit to look at our shadows, to accept them as part of who we are, without judgment. This is your divine work —the work of turning darkness into light.

Transmuting the shadow is not only a personal duty but a collective one. By working on yourself, you work on the world.

Acceptance of misery is key, but it doesn't mean succumbing to it. Instead, it means working actively to make the world a little less miserable. You begin by making yourself whole.

Reflect on this:

> "We all carry shadows within us. To claim otherwise is either a lie or a sign that one remains unconscious of their deeper self—this simply means the initiation has yet to occur.
>
> The moment of initiation is when the veil lifts, revealing these shadows for what they are. Once this happens, the choice is yours:
>
> Will you manipulate the world through the shadow's influence, or will you undertake the sacred work of transmuting that energy and healing it?"

The shadow is not your enemy. It is a teacher, waiting for you to recognize its lessons. To work with the shadow is to embark on a path of deep <u>alchemy</u>—the alchemy of the soul.

When you face it, you transform ignorance into wisdom, darkness into light, and separation into unity. This is the real work. This is the journey toward liberation.

Now, ask yourself: What shadow resides within you? What have you been avoiding, or what are you too afraid to face? It's time to look within, to see the shadow for what it truly is, and begin the work of transmuting it.

This is not only your personal task but an essential part of your existence. You may also see these shadows reflected in others.

Rather than reacting or trying to control them, strengthen your own inner anchor.

Give them space to grow, just as you give yourself space to evolve. Non-attachment is essential. Accept and observe the shadow, whether it is within you or in others, with the light of consciousness.

Allow it to be seen without judgment or identification. This is one of the ways true transformation and healing can take place.

If it feels appropriate, have a conversation with yourself or with the other person about the shadow. Do this with the intention of reducing suffering and bringing awareness, accepting that suffering is part of life. The goal is to alleviate misery, not to add to it.

The aim is not to judge, but to bring awareness to the shadow, so that both parties can move toward growth and transformation.

Uniting the Psyche

The path to transcending the shadows begins with The Noble Eightfold Path—a guide to liberation, not just from external suffering, but from the internal chains of the mind.

This path is not a set of moral rules but a roadmap to the evolution of consciousness, urging us to rise above the cycle of ego, desire, and fear that keeps us bound to the lower planes of existence.

The pendulum swing of life—between joy and sorrow, light and dark—is inevitable. Yet, we are not bound to its lower arcs. We must ascend to a higher plane of consciousness, where the dualities cease to dominate us.

- **1. Right Understanding**: Know the nature of reality. Suffering is not something we escape; it's something we transcend by understanding its source. Attachment to the egoic self, to the symbols and stories of the material world, is the root of all misery. We must see beyond the illusions.

- **2. Right Intention**: Purify your will. Align your desires not with material gains or fleeting pleasures but with the inner work of uniting the psyche. It's the psyche's fragmentation that manifests as chaos and destruction—wars within, wars without.

- **3. Right Speech**: Words are spells. Every word carries vibration, and each vibration can either bind us further to the shadows or liberate us. Speak with the clarity of truth, with words that dissolve illusion, not strengthen it.

- **4. Right Action**: Every movement of the body should be a dance in harmony with the higher Self. The physical is not separate from the spiritual; it is an extension. Shamanic dances, those ancient rituals, were a reset for the psyche—a way to unite what was fragmented. In our modern age, that connection is lost, and the energy, instead of transforming, festers into shadow.

- **5. Right Livelihood**: How you live, how you eat, how you exist—all of it affects your vibration. You cannot ascend in mind if your life is rooted in actions that degrade your spirit. Your work, your relationships, your environment must support the journey upward.

- **6. Right Effort**: The work is continual. The process is fall and get back up again. Life will knock you down; the shadows will reappear. But each time, you rise, stronger, more awake, more aligned with the higher Self. This is the alchemical process of transforming lead into gold, shadow into light.

- **7. Right Mindfulness**: Observe. The mind is a battlefield, where shadows and light constantly fight for dominance. But the key is to step back, to become the witness. Watch the pendulum swing, but do not be swept away by it. Remain anchored in the present, above the mental games of the ego.

- **8. Right Concentration**: Focus your mind. The ego will try to pull you into distractions, into endless cycles of desire, but your work is to sharpen your focus, to concentrate on the ultimate goal—unity, wholeness, the return to the formless.

We are living in a time of spiritual, mental, and physical crisis. The shadow energies that remain unprocessed within us are manifesting outwardly as wars, divisions, and global turmoil.

Religion, which once held the keys to these mysteries, has become stagnant. The symbols that were once gateways to the divine have been taken literally, worshiped as ends in themselves.

But symbols are merely pointers, signposts toward the unmanifested, the formless God.

We must stop worshiping the symbols and start understanding what they represent. The path is not through blind faith but through direct experience of the divine, the formless, the eternal.

The psyche must be united, for it is this split—between mind and spirit, ego and soul—that creates suffering. Techniques that once seemed strange—shamanic dances, rituals, ecstatic practices—were designed to unite these fragments, to heal the rift within.

When we lose these practices, we lose the reset, the balance. The energy gets stuck, and what should have been transformed into light is released as darkness—wars, destruction, and division.

Incorporating the Dionysian spirit offers a way to engage with the shadows in a manner that promotes release, not destruction. The ecstatic rituals of the ancients were small resets—adult ways of allowing the psyche to vent its energy in ethical, conscious ways.

Through dance, music, and ecstatic expression, we can release the shadows that build up inside us, preventing them from festering into chaos or inner division.

Yet, even in these moments of release, we must understand that no external pleasure, no wild abandon, can fill the deep void we all carry. Only by confronting that void—by knowing the vast emptiness within—can we learn to find true joy.

This is the paradox: only by diving into the nothingness do we realize that contentment, true satisfaction, can only come from within, from embracing the void rather than fearing it.

Many people live trapped in a low-vibration, ego-driven state of mind, unaware of the unconscious shadows and toxic behaviors they carry. These behaviors are often rooted in fear, guilt, and the unhealed wounds of the inner child.

They cannot embrace the Dionysian spirit—true ecstatic release—because they are fixated on ownership, seeking safety and worth in controlling and possessing.

This leads to an imbalance where, on one side, there is the empath, consumed by others' pain, and on the other side, the narcissist, blind to their own.

Both remain unaware of their condition, living out these extremes without knowing who they are. But if we bring conscious awareness to our behaviors, we begin to break the chains of these unconscious patterns.

Slowly, we can see that no gods are waiting to punish us, and the rigid laws we think we must follow are not commandments to be obeyed but invitations to recognize the interconnectedness of all things in the universe, an interconnectedness based on love, not control.

This essence of interconnectedness is something we can only truly grasp when we experience both extremes—the light and the shadow—and learn to hold them both in our psyche. This is the Hermetic Principle of polarity: opposites are part of the same whole.

When we reconcile these extremes within ourselves, we reach a higher state of consciousness, where we dance with life instead of resisting it, understanding that judgment is not our task. The universal laws are already in place to maintain balance.

Our role is simply to live, learn, and evolve.

All mystics understand that desires are endless, the cycles of craving and suffering are endless, and even the pursuit of Dionysian pleasures eventually leads to a deeper truth.

When all desires have been exhausted and every extreme has been experienced, what remains is the nothingness—the void. This void is not a place of resistance or a split in the psyche, but the profound realization of the Self.

It is from this space of emptiness, this deep understanding of our true nature, that compassion flows naturally, unforced and unbound, as we finally recognize the interconnectedness of all life beyond the illusions of ego and desire.

The crisis we face now is a call for one more Prometheus, one more Lucifer—the bringer of light, the one who dares to defy the stagnation of society and bring knowledge, awareness, and transformation.

We are on the brink of another deluge, but it was never the physical waters of the Earth that were the true threat.

The flood has always been symbolic—a deluge of our own shadows, the unprocessed pain, fear, and ego that have accumulated over centuries.

Water, in ancient symbols, never referred to literal floods, but to the depths of the unconscious, the emotional and spiritual crises we avoid. The real danger is not external but within—an overflow of suppressed darkness.

To prevent being consumed by these forces, we must face and transmute our shadows, allowing the symbolic waters to cleanse and transform us, rather than letting them overwhelm and drown us.

Now is the time for a new awakening. To rise above fear, guilt, and the shadows of the mind. We must reclaim the divine spark within and remember that we are the creators of our reality.

Ascend the egoistic mind, unite the psyche, and bring light where there is darkness. The transformation begins within, and from that inner alchemy, the world will change.

The time for a new fire is now.

The Anchor

The body is the field, and the Self is the knower of the field. The goal of life is to understand this distinction. Through knowledge, discernment, and consistent practice, one can minimize suffering, though complete liberation is not possible in this world.

The aim is to reduce suffering as much as possible, while recognizing the inherent limitations of human existence.

Understanding the Field and the Knower

"The body is the temple of the soul, but it is perishable, transient, and subject to decay."

"The Self is neither born nor does it die; it is eternal and changeless."

"The Knower is awareness; it is not the content of awareness."

The body is the home of the soul, and both are interlinked. The body is the field, but the Self is the knower of the field. We need to understand this distinction to live wisely.

Just because the body is temporary doesn't mean it shouldn't be cared for—it is sacred. The soul lives within it, but the soul is not bound by it.

The body will wither, emotions will rise and fall, but the Self remains untouched.

Think of it like a person driving a car. You maintain the car, fuel it, keep it in good shape, but you know you are not the car.

The car helps you move through the world, but it's just a vehicle. Similarly, the body allows the soul to experience life, but it's not the essence of who we are.

When we experience pain, whether physical or emotional, we can pause and remember:

> "This is not me; I am the one observing this."

The knower, the soul, witnesses all but remains untouched. Detachment doesn't mean disconnection; it means seeing clearly, not being lost in the temporary. As the Upanishads teach,

> "You are the infinite, clothed in the finite."

Modern tools like CBT echo this ancient wisdom. When anxiety or sadness arise, they suggest recognizing these emotions as passing clouds in the sky of awareness. You are the sky, not the clouds. Don't fight the feelings—acknowledge them, but know they will pass.

Living this way doesn't mean neglecting the material world. The spiritual and material are two sides of the same coin. The soul is in the body, so we care for both.

This balance is the art of living—engaging fully in life while staying rooted in the awareness that we are more than the sum of our physical and mental parts.

To deepen this understanding, we must also recognize the flow of emotions as natural, like waves on the surface of the ocean. These emotional currents rise and fall, but beneath them, the deeper Self remains steady, like the ocean's still depths.

By staying anchored in this awareness, we can allow emotions to move without being swept away. This is the foundation of spiritual practice—establishing an inner anchor that keeps us rooted in the unchanging truth, even as life's emotional tides come and go.

It is this inner grounding that prepares us for the sacred dialogue with the universe.

Observe the emotional vibrations as they rise and fall—that is their function. Yet, the cosmic laws remain constant, always in operation, regardless of these fluctuations.

A practitioner must establish their own anchor, a personal law forged through practice. Over time, this becomes their microcosmic law, guiding them through life without being swayed by the emotional tides.

This anchor allows one to flow with life without guilt, letting energy move freely. By putting intentions out into the universe, and listening for its response, we enter the sacred dialogue — micro to macro, macro to micro. The universe listens, and so must we, attuning ourselves to its wisdom.

The distinction between body and Self isn't about escape; it's about perspective. You take care of the body because it's the vehicle, but you remain centered in the truth that the soul is beyond.

Command:

Understand that you are not your thoughts, emotions, or body. You are the witness to them. Do not confuse your identity with your field of experiences.

Mastering the Modifications of the Field

Desires arise within the field. They are impermanent and bring suffering when pursued without discernment. As stated in the Bhagavad Gita (13:6):

> "Desire, aversion, pleasure, and pain — these are the modifications of the field."

From Stoicism:

> "It is not events that disturb people, but their judgments about them."

The same principle applies to desire. The unwise pursuit of pleasure leads to dissatisfaction. The wise see through its fleeting nature.

Desire-driven behavior leads to maladaptive patterns. Mindfulness-based practices help detach from the automatic responses to pleasure and pain. This is necessary to cultivate inner peace.

Desires, when pursued without wisdom, can never truly satisfy us. We fulfill one, and another arises. It's an endless loop, and deep down, we know this.

No matter how many desires we satisfy, the void remains—the space within that no external thing can fill. The more we chase pleasure, the more we confront this emptiness. This is the nature of human existence.

Existentially, this void is not something to fear; it's the doorway to understanding. The endless pursuit of desire distracts us from the deeper truth that we are more than our wants, more than our fleeting cravings. As Jean-Paul Sartre said,

> "Man is condemned to be free; because once thrown into the world, he is responsible for everything he does."

Our freedom to desire without end creates a cycle of dissatisfaction until we confront the deeper truth—there's no fulfillment in desire, only in the Self.

What fills that emptiness is not more—it's less. It's the realization that we are complete, not through things, but through being.

And within this understanding arises compassion—first for ourselves, for having misunderstood what it means to be whole, and then for others, seeing them entangled in the same illusion.

At the core, we are not separate individuals living isolated lives, but interconnected expressions of one source, one reality. This understanding echoes both ancient wisdom and modern science.

Quantum physics suggests that everything in the universe is deeply connected at a subatomic level, forming an inseparable web of energy and matter. The mystics have long said the same:

there is no true separation between you and the rest of existence.

Leibniz's concept of the *monad* is central to his philosophy of unity. He believed that monads are the fundamental, indivisible units of reality, like atoms of existence, but they are not physical — they are metaphysical, representing the essence of all things.

Each monad, while being unique, contains within it a complete reflection of the entire universe. As he put it,

"Each monad reflects the entire universe in its own way."

This means that every monad, though distinct, is intimately connected to the whole, and nothing exists in isolation.

In simple terms, each individual — each monad — carries within it the totality of existence, even though we may perceive ourselves as separate beings. This reflects the unity of all things: each part contains the whole.

Even though we appear separate, we are interconnected at the deepest level. Our experiences, desires, and thoughts may be unique, but they are all part of a universal structure.

The boundaries we perceive between ourselves and others are illusions. The Self is not a mere drop in the ocean — it is the entire ocean, compressed into a single drop. You carry the totality of existence within you, and so does everyone else.

When we truly grasp this unity, compassion naturally flows, because to harm another is to harm oneself. To love another is to love oneself.

This realization transforms how we relate to the world, dissolving selfishness and replacing it with a profound understanding that we are all part of a singular, interconnected whole.

The void we feel isn't a lack; it's a misperception — a misunderstanding of the completeness that already exists within us.

Deeper love and compassion arise, not out of fear of hell or desire for heaven, but because of an innate understanding of our interconnectedness. This compassion isn't transactional; it doesn't depend on rewards or punishments.

It comes from the realization that, at the deepest level, there is no separation between us and others. When we act with kindness, it is not because we expect something in return, but because we recognize that in helping another, we are ultimately helping ourselves.

This love is grounded in the truth that all existence is one. As we begin to see ourselves in others and others in ourselves, compassion naturally blossoms. The motivation for doing good shifts from personal gain to the joy of expressing our shared humanity.

We no longer avoid harm out of fear, but because we understand that harm done to another is harm done to the whole, and we are part of that whole. This is the root of self-realization: to see the unity of all life and to act in harmony with that truth.

This realization dissolves the illusion of separation. There's no "me" chasing fulfillment outside, no "others" who are different from us. It's all one. The emptiness we feel isn't a lack; it's the space where unity is revealed.

When we see that, we stop searching for satisfaction through desires and begin to live in a deeper, more connected way.

This is where true peace is found—not in the fulfillment of desire, but in the dissolution of the belief that we are separate from everything else.

Command:

Observe your desires without acting on them. Understand their temporary nature. Practice detachment by focusing on long-term well-being rather than short-term gratification.

Dissolving Ego and False Identity

The ego is an illusion within the field, a false construct that creates a sense of separation between you and others. It thrives on attachment to your personal identity, leading to suffering.

The Bhagavad Gita (13:7) teaches the importance of freeing yourself from egoism by recognizing the inherent flaws of life — birth, death, aging, disease, and pain.

Understanding these realities helps to weaken the ego's grip and reduces the suffering it causes.

The Upanishads teach that ego is the illusion (maya) that keeps the self bound to the cycle of rebirth. The Isha Upanishad states:

"He who sees all beings in his own self, and his own self in all beings, loses all fear and attachment."

By practicing the ability to see yourself in others and others in yourself, you begin to dissolve the boundaries the ego creates. This shift in perspective reduces attachment because you no longer view yourself as separate and distinct from others.

In modern psychological terms, the ego refers to the part of the mind that creates a sense of individual identity — who we think we are. It helps us navigate the world by forming a self-concept based on our thoughts, memories, and experiences.

However, this constructed identity is limited and often rigid, creating a false sense of separateness.

Freud referred to the ego as the "reality principle," guiding us in daily interactions, but even he acknowledged the tension between the ego and deeper aspects of the psyche — the unconscious, where the true self resides.

This false identity, or ego, thrives on attachment to roles, labels, and external validation. It gives rise to the illusion that our worth is tied to what we achieve, how we are perceived, and what we possess.

The philosopher Alan Watts echoed this in his work, saying,

> "The ego is nothing other than the focus of conscious attention."

This focus can blind us to the larger reality that we are part of something greater, creating an illusion of separation.

Esoteric wisdom calls this illusion *maya*, as mentioned in the Upanishads, which traps us in the cycle of suffering by making us identify solely with our personal experiences, desires, and fears.

Carl Jung also spoke about the need to transcend the ego to reach what he called individuation—the process of becoming whole by integrating the conscious and unconscious parts of ourselves.

When we identify less with the ego and more with the deeper Self—what Jung called the collective unconscious—we begin to see beyond the narrow confines of individuality. We become more aware of our interconnectedness with others and the universe as a whole.

From both a psychological and philosophical perspective, the dissolution of the ego doesn't mean destroying it. The ego is a necessary tool for functioning in the world, but it must be put in its proper place.

In Freudian psychology, the ego mediates between the Self and reality, but it is a limited and conditioned construct. Identifying too strongly with the ego leads to neurosis and anxiety. Liberation from the ego is necessary for mental clarity and fulfillment.

In the words of Eckhart Tolle,

> "The ego loves to strengthen itself by complaining. The ego loves to be right. But in dissolving the ego, we come to a place where we don't need to be right, or special—we just need to be."

> **Command:**
>
> Stop identifying with the ego. Understand that it is a false construct. Practice seeing yourself in others and others in yourself. This reduces attachment, fear, and desire for control.

Cultivating Non-Attachment and Equanimity

Non-attachment is the foundation of self-mastery. The Bhagavad Gita (13:9) emphasizes detachment from sons, wife, and home, and remaining even-minded in both pleasing and unpleasing events.

I understand this may seem like a controversial topic, but with time and experience, one realizes the truth of this. No one is the owner of anything or anyone. You and others don't own each other. One can be a guardian, helper, or lover, but never the owner.

Non-attachment doesn't mean abandoning your duties. As the Bhagavad Gita teaches,

> "You are qualified simply with regard to action, never with regard to its results. You must be neither motivated by the results of action nor attached to inaction." (2:47).

You must fulfill your responsibilities, but without becoming attached to the outcomes or letting your ego dictate control over others.

Just reflect on how often your own ego plays you, pushing you to control someone else's outcome, driven by the desire for validation, power, or ownership. This creates endless suffering, for yourself and others.

It's better, in fact, to not get married and have children. This, too, may seem controversial, but time will teach you the value of this realization.

The institution of marriage, in its traditional sense, stopped working long ago and often leads to more suffering due to attachment and expectations. If you are not married, don't rush into it. Non-attachment is far easier to cultivate when you're free from those societal pressures.

However, if you are already married and have children, that is your place. You are exactly where you are meant to be. Your dharma now is to perform your duties as a spouse or parent, but with non-attachment.

Love them deeply, but without clinging to the idea that you control their paths or that they belong to you. You are a guardian, not an owner. In this way, you can minimize suffering and perform your duties with clarity and peace.

This is not to say that you should avoid relationships altogether. Instead, learn about life, the human psyche, and your own inner workings before entering into relationships.

Relationships built on societal constructs like marriage, often tied to control, ownership, and outdated expectations, are no longer compatible with the new age of consciousness.

The relationships we need now are based on mutual understanding, where two individuals come together as mature adults, free to explore boundaries with respect and consent.

Non-attachment does not mean withdrawing from the world. It means participating fully, but without the baggage of ego-driven desires, fear, or unconscious patterns.

Engage with life, with people, and with relationships, but do so without the shadows of ownership, insecurity, or control. Understand that life is transient, that nothing is permanent, and that this very transience is what gives life its depth and beauty.

Approach everything with maturity and conscious awareness. Don't let your unresolved shadows play you. Instead, shine the light of consciousness on your actions and relationships.

Realize that no one owns anyone—each person is sovereign unto themselves within the greater unity of existence. In that understanding, there is space for real love, trust, and growth.

Mature relationships are those that promote personal and spiritual growth without judgment or control. They are relationships built on understanding, mutual support, and respect.

They are free from guilt, fear, lack, and the chains of societal dogma or state-owned powers. These are the relationships worth nurturing—the ones where two souls walk together in love, not out of obligation, but out of a deep and conscious choice to grow alongside one another.

The Bhagavad Gita aligns with the teaching of the Stoic philosopher Epictetus:

"Some things are up to us, others are not."

Focusing on what we can control, and that is your inner strength, your anchor with the Self, the non-attachment, cultivates equanimity.

"You always own the option of having no opinion. There is never any need to get worked up or to trouble your soul about things you can't control. These things are not asking to be judged by you. Leave them alone."

— Marcus Aurelius, Meditations

The wisdom in Marcus Aurelius' quote offers a powerful tool for empaths, encouraging them to release unnecessary judgments and emotional attachments to things beyond their control. By practicing this detachment, empaths can protect their sensitive souls from being overwhelmed.

However, the irony lies in the fact that while empaths quote this advice as a guide for emotional boundaries, it is often narcissists and manipulative individuals who live by it effortlessly.

A word of advice: when you begin practicing detachment, you may often fall from detachment into guilt, and it can feel overwhelming. Don't worry about it. With time, practice, wisdom, and discernment, you will learn and grow.

Start small—treat it like a game, perhaps trying detachment for just one hour as a playful exercise, and then gradually increase the duration. Remember, falling and rising again is part of the process—that's how it goes.

Mindfulness and Acceptance and Commitment Therapy (ACT) share a common emphasis on being present and accepting reality without becoming overly attached or reactive to it.

- **Mindfulness** involves being fully aware of the present moment, observing thoughts, emotions, and sensations without judgment. Instead of trying to avoid or control uncomfortable feelings, mindfulness encourages us to simply notice and accept them, which prevents overreaction or becoming overwhelmed by them.

- **Acceptance and Commitment Therapy (ACT)** takes this a step further by not only encouraging acceptance of the present moment but also fostering psychological flexibility. This means the ability to adapt to changing circumstances, even when faced with distress or discomfort. ACT encourages people to commit to actions that align with their values, even in the face of challenging emotions.

Both approaches highlight the importance of not clinging to the moment or trying to change what is out of your control.

Instead, embracing the present without resistance promotes emotional resilience—the capacity to recover from difficulties and face challenges without being emotionally drained.

In essence, this acceptance creates a mental space where you can respond to life's difficulties more effectively, without becoming rigid or overly attached to outcomes, thus fostering well-being.

> **Command:**
>
> Remain detached from both success and failure. Do not let external circumstances disturb your inner peace. Accept life as it comes, and act with wisdom rather than reactivity.

Seeking Knowledge of the Self

True knowledge is understanding the nature of the Self and the field. The Gita (13:11) states:

> "Constancy in knowledge of what relates to the Self, perceiving the purpose of knowledge of reality—this is knowledge."

The Self represents the eternal soul, the pure consciousness within us, while the field refers to the physical body and the material world, including our mind and senses.

The Gita teaches that it is essential to know the difference between these two: the unchanging Self and the ever-changing material existence.

In verse 13:11, Lord Krishna emphasizes the importance of constancy in this knowledge—meaning, keeping a steady awareness of the true nature of the Self without getting confused by the distractions of the material world.

This steady knowledge helps us stay grounded in our spiritual understanding and not be overly attached to the temporary nature of life.

The verse also talks about understanding the purpose of seeking this knowledge. True knowledge isn't just about collecting facts or ideas; it's about knowing why we are seeking this understanding in the first place.

It could be to achieve inner peace, spiritual growth, or liberation. When we understand the purpose of knowledge, we can apply it meaningfully in our lives.

The Upanishads emphasize that liberation comes from the knowledge of the Self (Atman) and its unity with Brahman. The Chandogya Upanishad proclaims:

"Tat tvam asi" ("Thou art That") — the individual self is the universal Self.

Psychological research shows that self-awareness and introspection are key to mental health. The practice of reflection and meditation allows one to separate from automatic thoughts and reactions, fostering deeper understanding.

The journey to answering the question Who am I? is the key that unlocks the door to dissolving false identity and awakening the true Self. This ancient quest has echoed through the ages, inscribed on the temple of Delphi:

"Know thyself, and thou shalt know the universe and the gods."

To know oneself is to recognize that the boundaries between you and the universe are an illusion; the deeper you go within, the more you realize that you are not separate from the cosmos but a reflection of it.

This question, Who am I?, peels away the layers of false identity — the ego, the roles you play, the labels you've adopted over the years. The mind has been programmed to identify with these external things: career, relationships, societal expectations.

But the essence of who you truly are goes far beyond these transient identities. The pursuit of self-knowledge is not about adding more to your life — more achievements, more possessions — but about subtracting what is false, what doesn't resonate with your true nature.

Modern wisdom aligns with this. We live in a world that tells us to chase everything — success, validation, and material gain. But the seeker understands that the only thing worth pursuing is what aligns with your deeper self, your true path.

This requires a certain kind of discernment: not every opportunity is meant for you, not every desire is yours to follow. Align with what feels true, what speaks to your soul, and let go of the rest. In this way, you walk your unique path, one that no one else can walk for you.

Deprogramming the limitations imposed by the mind begins with recognizing that much of our thinking is conditioned. From childhood, we inherit beliefs, fears, and desires from society, family, and culture that may not reflect our true self.

To dissolve these, meditation and self-inquiry are key. In silence, the mind begins to quiet, and you can observe the thoughts, seeing them for what they are—just thoughts, not you.

As you ask, Who am I?, these layers of mental conditioning start to dissolve, and you begin to tap into the deeper intelligence of intuition.

Intuition, that inner knowing, is the divine instrument that guides you on your path. It is the voice of the soul speaking through the noise of the mind. To build it, you must learn to trust it and listen to its whispers, which often come when the mind is quiet.

When you stop overthinking, you begin to hear the subtle guidance of the universe moving through you.

The mind, when deprogrammed from its limitations, becomes a powerful tool for higher understanding. It can then perceive reality as it is, not as it has been conditioned to see.

To ascend the mind is to rise above the conditioning of fear, scarcity, and control and instead operate from a place of clarity and truth. In this state, the divine instrument—the mind, body, and soul—works in harmony, attuned to the flow of the universe.

As you journey into this deeper knowing, you realize that the divine has been within you all along. You are not separate from the universe, but a manifestation of it.

The more you know yourself, the more you align with the vast intelligence that underlies all of existence. Tat tvam asi—"Thou art That."

You are the universe discovering itself, and through self-knowledge, the illusions of separation fall away.

> **Command:**
>
> Pursue self-knowledge relentlessly. Engage in meditation, self-reflection, and study of sacred texts. Seek to understand your true nature beyond the body and mind.

Surrender and Devotion

Surrendering to a higher power dissolves ego and liberates the Self. The Gita (13:10) encourages unswerving devotion to the divine through exclusive yogic discipline.

The concept of surrender is echoed in the Upanishads and mystical traditions. In the Bhagavad Gita (18:66), Krishna says:

> "Abandon all varieties of dharma and just surrender unto Me. I will deliver you from all sins; do not fear."

It is important, however, to create your own sense of devotion to the divine, one that resonates with your heart. Stay away from any form of dogma or rigid structures that limit your spiritual expression.

Instead, focus on the essence of devotion—connecting with the divine beyond rituals of guilt or obligation. True surrender comes from the purity of intention, not from external rules, allowing you to cultivate a relationship with the divine that is freeing and uplifting.

Surrender to the flow of life. We cannot control everything, and acceptance of the unknown is key. Just like the North Star guides travelers, our North Node—our soul's purpose—guides us, if we trust in it.

The truth is that, despite all challenges, love ultimately prevails. Even in destruction, life finds a way to bloom again.

The deeper journey of healing begins with consciousness—knowing and embracing your own shadows, the wounded child within.

This is personal work, often done alone, but necessary. Only after healing yourself can you truly blossom and share love outwardly with the world.

Never disown yourself. Break through mental barriers that keep you stuck. The path forward requires self-acceptance, self-compassion, and an understanding that the journey, though solitary at times, leads to a greater connection with others and the universe.

When we heal and become whole, we contribute to the larger unity of existence, spreading love and light naturally.

In psychological terms, surrendering control refers to releasing the need to manage or dictate every aspect of life, especially things outside of one's influence. This is important because the desire for control often stems from anxiety—the fear of uncertainty or the unknown.

When we constantly try to control outcomes, people, or situations, it creates mental tension and stress, as many factors in life are inherently unpredictable.

Mindfulness-based therapies, such as Acceptance and Commitment Therapy (ACT) and Mindfulness-Based Stress Reduction (MBSR), emphasize letting go of this need for control.

These approaches teach that resisting or trying to control every thought, emotion, or event in life only increases suffering.

Instead, mindfulness encourages individuals to observe thoughts and feelings without judgment and accept situations as they are, without the need to fix or change them.

From a psychological perspective, this practice of surrendering control reduces anxiety by shifting focus from trying to control external outcomes to managing internal responses.

When individuals realize that many things are beyond their control—such as how others behave or how situations unfold—they can redirect their energy toward what they can influence: their own reactions, attitudes, and emotional responses.

For example, in a stressful situation, the anxious mind wants to plan for every possible outcome or micromanage the situation to avoid discomfort. However, this often leads to frustration because complete control is impossible.

By practicing mindfulness and learning to surrender control, individuals can reduce anxiety by accepting uncertainty. This approach fosters psychological well-being by promoting resilience, emotional flexibility, and a sense of inner calm.

As a result, individuals experience less mental strain and more peace as they learn to navigate life's unpredictability with a balanced, adaptive mindset.

Command:

Surrender your ego and sense of personal control to the higher Self. Practice devotion, not just through rituals, but through the total renunciation of personal desire and attachment.

Seeing the Unity in All Beings

The wise person sees the Lord equally present in all beings. The Gita (13:27) states:

"He who sees the Supreme Lord as situated equally in all creatures, not perishing when they perish, he sees."

The Upanishads declare:

"Sarvam khalvidam brahma"—all this is Brahman.

This teaching asserts the oneness of all existence. Division is an illusion born from ignorance. "Verily all this is the Brahman". It is considered to be the sum of all Veda and Vedanta.

In simple terms, Brahman is the ultimate reality, the source of everything that exists. It is the unchanging, eternal essence that underlies the entire universe.

According to the ancient teachings of the Upanishads and the Bhagavad Gita, Brahman is not separate from the world; it is the world, and beyond it. Everything we see, hear, feel, and experience is an expression of Brahman.

Brahman is often described as formless, infinite, and beyond our limited understanding. It is present in every being and every part of the universe.

When the Gita says that the wise person sees the Supreme Lord equally in all beings, it means that someone who understands Brahman sees no division between people, creatures, or things— everything is connected and part of the same divine essence.

In essence, Brahman is the unity behind all diversity, the one reality that manifests in countless forms. Understanding this dissolves the illusion of separation, leading to the realization that we are all part of this greater whole.

"All is Brahman" simply means that all existence is one and interconnected, no matter how it appears on the surface.

The Dance of Hide and Seek

I found you after a painful journey,
A path woven with sorrow and strife,
I embraced you after the dark night,
Where shadows danced with the edge of life.

I cried with you after the long separateness,
As if the stars had shattered in their fall,
Yet, in our reunion, a fleeting breath—
You hide again, as is your call.

The play of hide and seek began anew,
But this time, I did not forget,
For I've seen the truth within your veil,
And yet, the play is not over yet.

Your dance is my command to follow,
Your rhythm is the pulse of my soul,
The game must go on, the drama must unfold,
As your play is my life, my ultimate goal.

Until next time, until beyond time,
Where there's no longer an "until" at all,
We will meet again, once and for all,
In the silence where the veils forever fall.

In that moment, we shall be as one,
No more hiding, no more night,
Just the endless dance of the Divine,
In the boundless space of eternal void.

Empathy and compassion are central to psychological health because they allow us to connect deeply with others and recognize the shared human experience of suffering.

When we truly understand that all people experience pain, challenges, and emotional struggles in various forms, it opens the door to genuine connection.

This shared awareness reduces feelings of isolation and helps dissolve self-centeredness, which often comes from believing our suffering is unique or greater than others'.

By recognizing that suffering is universal, we are more inclined to help each other rather than add to the burden of suffering through judgment, indifference, or harmful actions.

When we extend compassion, we break the cycle of hurt and negativity, creating space for healing and support.

Instead of perpetuating suffering, we can actively work to alleviate it—both in ourselves and in others—by fostering understanding, kindness, and solidarity.

This simple act of helping each other creates a ripple effect, contributing to the collective well-being of humanity.

Command:

See the divine in all beings. Treat everyone as an extension of yourself. Understand that all distinctions—race, gender, status—are superficial. Only the one Self exists in all.

The Hermetic Path

In the Hermetic philosophy, the universe is seen as a living mind, where all beings are interconnected, and everything happens for the purpose of spiritual evolution.

This world is not simply a place to live out mundane experiences; it is a sacred school for the soul, designed to help us elevate to our higher selves.

The journey of life is one of learning, unlearning, and transmutation, as we are continually presented with opportunities to grow, transcend, and evolve.

At the core of Hermetic teachings is the principle of mental transmutation—the ability to transform lower states of consciousness into higher ones.

Let's look at the common Hermetic laws, often referred to as the Seven Hermetic Principles, described in simple terms:

The Principle of Mentalism:

- Everything in the universe is a product of the mind. The universe itself is like a vast, living mind, and all things exist as thoughts within it. This means that what we experience in life begins with our thoughts, and by changing how we think, we can change our reality.

The Principle of Correspondence:

- As above, so below; as below, so above. This principle explains that there is harmony and connection between different levels of reality. The patterns we see in the physical world reflect higher, spiritual truths, and vice versa. For example, the way the cosmos operates mirrors the way our inner world functions.

The Principle of Vibration:

- Everything is in constant motion, nothing is truly still. Everything vibrates at different levels—whether it's a rock, a thought, or a feeling. Higher vibrations are associated with positive, uplifting energy, while lower vibrations are tied to negativity. By raising our vibration through thought, emotion, or action, we can improve our experiences.

The Principle of Polarity:

- Everything has two sides, or poles—like hot and cold, light and dark. These opposites are actually the same thing at different degrees. Understanding this helps us see that opposites are connected, and by shifting perspective, we can change how we feel about a situation.

The Principle of Rhythm:

- Life moves in cycles, like the ebb and flow of the tides. There are times of growth and times of rest, highs and lows. This principle reminds us that everything has a rhythm, and we can learn to flow with life's natural cycles rather than resisting them.

The Principle of Cause and Effect:

- Nothing happens by chance. Every action has a reaction, and everything that happens has a cause. By understanding this, we can take responsibility for our actions and recognize that we create our reality through our thoughts, decisions, and actions.

The Principle of Gender:

- Everything has both masculine and feminine energy. This doesn't necessarily refer to biological gender but rather to the balance of active (masculine) and receptive (feminine) forces within us and in the world. Both energies are necessary for creation and harmony.

These principles are meant to guide us in understanding how the universe operates, and how we can align ourselves with these natural laws to achieve spiritual growth and harmony in life.

Just as alchemists turn base metals into gold, we are called to transmute our inner shadows into light, integrating them into our consciousness for healing and growth.

These shadows, often the source of our suffering, are not meant to be rejected or hidden but embraced as stepping stones to higher awareness.

The 21 shadows listed are common aspects of human experience, deeply rooted in the ego, which can distort our perception and disconnect us from our true divine nature.

These shadows—such as pride, fear, anger, shame, and jealousy—are invitations to reflect on the parts of ourselves that need healing.

By working on them, both within ourselves and recognizing them in others, we begin the process of inner alchemy.

Here are 21 shadows you can choose to work on, and the higher virtues they can be transmuted into, each holding the potential for healing and growth:

1:

Pride – The illusion of superiority, masking insecurity.

Transmute into: **Humility** – Recognizing the divinity in all and honoring equality.

2:

Fear – The false belief that we are separate from the source of all.

Transmute into: **Courage** – Trusting in the unity and protection of divine energy.

3:

Anger – Unresolved pain, waiting to be acknowledged.

Transmute into: **Forgiveness** – Letting go of pain and embracing understanding.

4:

Jealousy – A projection of our own sense of lack.

Transmute into: **Contentment** – Recognizing abundance and celebrating others' success.

5:

Shame – The feeling of being unworthy, disconnected from divine love.

Transmute into: **Self-Worth** – Embracing the unconditional love of the divine.

6:

Guilt – Holding on to past actions, preventing healing and forgiveness.

Transmute into: **Self-Forgiveness** – Releasing the past and allowing healing.

7:

Control – The desire to dominate, fearing the flow of life.

Transmute into: **Surrender** – Trusting the natural flow of the universe.

8:

Greed – The endless craving for more, masking inner emptiness.

Transmute into: **Generosity** – Finding fulfillment in sharing and giving.

9:

Arrogance – The refusal to see others as mirrors of ourselves.

Transmute into: **Open-mindedness** – Recognizing wisdom in all beings.

10:

Self-Doubt – The shadow of not trusting in one's own divine power.

Transmute into: **Confidence** – Trusting in your inner divinity and purpose.

11:

Addiction – The compulsive escape from facing deeper emotions.

Transmute into: **Self-Mastery** – Cultivating discipline and emotional awareness.

12:

Judgment – Projecting one's own fears and flaws onto others.

Transmute into: **Compassion** – Understanding and accepting others as they are.

13:

Victimhood – Holding on to the belief that life happens to you, not for you.

Transmute into: **Empowerment** – Taking responsibility for your own growth and choices.

14:

Laziness – Avoiding responsibility, shying away from one's potential.

Transmute into: **Motivation** – Embracing your role in life's unfolding and your soul's work.

15:

Narcissism – Excessive self-focus that leads to emotional blindness.

Transmute into: **Empathy** – Expanding your awareness to include others' experiences.

16:

Self-Sabotage – Acting against one's own best interests due to fear of success.

Transmute into: **Self-Commitment** – Stepping into your full potential without fear.

17:

Perfectionism – The constant pursuit of flawlessness, masking fear of inadequacy.

Transmute into: **Self-Acceptance** – Recognizing your inherent worth as a divine being.

18:

Resentment – Clinging to old wounds, refusing to forgive.

Transmute into: **Release** – Letting go of past hurts to create space for healing.

> **19:**
>
> **Apathy** – Disconnection from emotions, preventing true engagement with life.
>
> *Transmute into*: **Passion** – Reconnecting with your emotional truth and living fully.

> **20:**
>
> **Over-Identification** – Confusing the ego's desires with the soul's purpose.
>
> *Transmute into*: **Soul Alignment** – Listening to the deeper calling of your higher self.

> **21:**
>
> **Intolerance** – Refusing to accept diversity, rejecting the interconnectedness of all beings.
>
> *Transmute into*: **Unity** – Embracing the divine in all forms and recognizing our oneness.

The process of transmutation is simple but requires deep commitment. First, we must acknowledge the shadow without judgment.

In Hermetic thought, the law of correspondence reminds us that everything outside is a reflection of what is inside. As the Kybalion states,

"As above, so below; as within, so without."

When we are triggered by anger, jealousy, or judgment in others, it's not simply an external issue. These emotions are signposts, reflecting shadows within us that need attention.

If we find ourselves disturbed by another's behavior, it is an opportunity to look within and see where those same traits may reside in our own psyche. The external world becomes a mirror for our internal state.

The work begins by recognizing these shadows. Through self-awareness and acceptance, we can begin to transmute them.

When we realize that these negative traits often stem from fear, insecurity, or the sense of separation from divine love, we can bring compassion and understanding to these parts of ourselves. This is how we begin to dissolve the ego's hold.

The Hermetic principle of *mentalism* teaches us that,

"The ALL is mind, the Universe is Mental."

Our thoughts shape our reality. Therefore, through the power of intention, meditation, and reflection, we can transform our shadows.

Understanding that these traits are not our true selves but are expressions of unresolved wounds allows us to step into our higher nature—the Higher Self, which is the part of us that is connected to divine wisdom and love.

Another Hermetic principle, the law of polarity, teaches that extremes can be balanced. Nothing is fixed, and opposites can be reconciled. Pride can be transmuted into humility, anger into forgiveness, and apathy into passion.

Every shadow contains within it the potential for its opposite virtue. By working with the energies of our shadows, we can transform what appears negative into a higher, more refined state of being.

This work is not just for personal evolution. When we transmute our shadows, we contribute to the collective awakening. The law of vibration teaches us that everything is energy. As we elevate our own vibration by healing the shadows within, we uplift those around us as well.

We begin to see the world and others through the lens of empathy and understanding, rather than judgment or fear. This creates ripples of healing that affect our relationships and communities, making us living examples of what it means to transcend the ego.

Remember, this world is a classroom—a place where the soul evolves by learning lessons of love, wisdom, and unity. By acknowledging and working on these 21 shadows, you not only elevate yourself but also help others along their path.

When you rise beyond the ego, you embody the divine light within, and in doing so, you fulfill your soul's purpose of evolving and returning to oneness with All.

Once you overcome your shadows—not by eliminating them, but by bringing the conscious light of awareness to them, accepting them without judgment, and understanding universal laws such as the law of karma—you begin to embody true freedom.

When you understand your shadows, they no longer control you. With this realization comes the ability to live in alignment with your higher will. As Aleister Crowley wrote,

> "Do what thou wilt shall be the whole of the Law. Love is the law, love under will."

This means living your life in harmony with your true purpose, guided by love, but always under the direction of your soul's higher will.

We all have limitations and shadows; this is part of being human. Take it easy on yourself and understand that all paths lead to the same destination. The journey is the true gift, not the destination.

Enjoy the process of growth, of learning, and of evolving into your true self.

"All religions are true, but all are imperfect in their own way. All paths lead to God."

The journey is not easy. In fact, it is the most difficult task one can undertake in this lifetime. But it is also the only truly worthwhile endeavor.

To stay on the path of growth and self-mastery, to continue following your bliss and not stray from your purpose, is the greatest achievement.

There will be moments of exhaustion, times when you feel lost or overwhelmed. But know that there are places to rest, points along the journey where you can rejuvenate your spirit before continuing on.

Keep moving forward. No matter which path you choose, as long as you are aware of your shadows and walking consciously, you are on the right path. The journey itself is the most noble pursuit, leading to true fulfillment and inner peace.

You will get everything, anything you desire, but you must be ready on that level of consciousness. Don't worry—you are exactly where you are supposed to be.

Life gives you every moment as an opportunity to learn and grow. Keep going, and trust the process.

Understand this: the journey is hard, the hardest thing one will ever face in this lifetime. But it is also true that to walk this path is the most noble task one can undertake.

The greatest mistake is to carry guilt for how far you've come. Do not carry guilt or fear, for the show is unfolding exactly as it should, and you are exactly where you are meant to be.

Ask yourself: What more do you seek to experience? Or is it enough? Not the kind of "enough" that arises from the shadows of pride, fear, or lack, but the kind of "enough" that comes when the soul whispers, I have experienced all there is, I have learned all I need.

That moment comes when nothing in this world can fill you any longer, when you realize that no manifested form can contain the vastness of your being, and no earthly boundary can confine your freedom.

That is when it is time to go home—when the soul realizes it is no longer confined by, nor can it be satisfied with, the limitations of physical forms, and yearns to return to its infinite, boundless source.

Command:

Walk this path without guilt or fear. The journey is difficult, but sacred. Trust the unfolding of the path. Sit, breathe, and burn in your shadows, allowing transformation to turn your inner lead into gold. Never abandon yourself, through this alchemy true freedom can be found.

If there's only one point you take from this guide, let it be this: Relax, breathe, observe, and don't get entangled. Everything will be revealed to you in time.

Good luck, and enjoy the show.

In Surrender, We Awaken

In the vastness of creation, those who came before us—close yet beyond reach—offer no answers. They too wandered, caught in the same cycle of seeking, reminding us that creation isn't a gift, but a challenge.

A call to rise above the illusions of ego, violence, and hate, which blind us to the unity that connects all.

Our path isn't about uncovering origins, but losing ourselves in the divine mystery.

The ego, the root of conflict, is a veil that separates us from Truth. When it dissolves, we shed our attachment to fear and division, leaving only light and oneness.

In surrender, we find unity—no creator, no created, only the One manifesting in infinite forms.

The myths reflect this eternal dance: to be created is to perish, and in this dissolution, we awaken to love, the true force that binds the universe.

"In the boundless expanse of creation, those who came before us whisper from afar, offering no answers, only the echo of their journey."

- This acknowledges the spiritual lineage or ancestors, often viewed as guides or previous seekers in mysticism. They offer a pathway but no definitive answers, as each soul's journey is individual.

"They wandered too, circling the same stars, reminding us that creation is not a gift, but a challenge to rise beyond ourselves."

- Mystical traditions often frame creation as a test or journey, where the soul must transcend the material and ego to reach higher understanding, not something passively received.

"It is a call to transcend the illusions of ego, hatred, and violence, for only in unity can we glimpse the truth that binds us all."

- This captures the mystical idea that ego, fear, and hate are obstacles to enlightenment. The "illusion" (Maya in some traditions) is what prevents the soul from recognizing divine unity.

"Our path is not in searching for beginnings, but in dissolving into the mystery of the divine, where all answers fade."

- Mysticism often emphasizes surrender and merging with the divine over intellectual understanding of origins. The soul's true quest is union with the Infinite, not just answers.

"The ego, like a veil of smoke, hides the Truth, blinding us to the light that waits behind the fog."

- The ego is frequently seen as the veil that obscures the divine or universal truth. Mystical traditions stress the dissolution of the ego as essential for enlightenment.

"When the veil of ego lifts, fear and division fall away, and all that remains is the brilliance of oneness."

- Once the ego dissolves, the soul can perceive its unity with all creation, a concept central to mystical experiences across traditions (Sufism's *Fana*, Advaita Vedanta's non-duality, etc.).

"In surrender, we find the secret: there is no creator, no created—only the One, endlessly unfolding in every form."

- This is a direct reference to the mystical experience of oneness, where distinctions between creator and creation fade, and only the divine presence, or unity, is perceived.

"The ancient stories are but reflections of an eternal dance: to be created is to fade away, and in that fading, we awaken to love, the force that holds the universe together."

- Myths in mysticism are often symbolic representations of cosmic truths. The idea of dissolution as a path to awakening aligns with the concept of *Fana* (annihilation of the ego self) or the mystical death that leads to rebirth in unity with the divine. Love, as the binding force, reflects many mystical traditions' focus on love as the highest form of divine connection.

The Dance of Unity

In the end, my friend, come back to the dance,
Where love moves freely, in every glance.
Taste the joy that unity brings,
Where the soul, unchained, spreads its wings.

Be compassionate, first to yourself,
Then to others—this is the true wealth.
For we are one, woven in light,
There is no other, no wrong, no right.

Cast away guilt, cast away shame,
These are illusions, they're not your name.
No fear in your heart, no burden to bear,
The universe holds you in infinite care.

Break the chains, rise above the mind,
The constructs of dogma, leave them behind.
Create a path that feels true to you,
And let others walk in their truth too.

Trust in the earth, trust in the sky,
In the magic of surrender, let yourself fly.
For in this letting go, love will appear,
To make this world better, right here, right near.

Dance with the stars, laugh with the sun,
You are not broken, you and the One.
In this unity, live without fear,
For love is the answer, always clear.

Harnessing Chaos

The myth of Phaethon is a powerful tale of ambition, failure, and the chaos that follows. Phaethon, the son of Helios, longed to prove himself and sought to ride his father's sun chariot across the sky.

Despite warnings of the dangers, Phaethon took the reins. As he soared higher, the horses sensed his inexperience, veering wildly. The sun chariot burned too hot, scorching the earth, causing fires, and plunging the world into chaos.

Seeing the destruction, Zeus struck Phaethon down with a thunderbolt to save the world from further disaster.

But in this myth lies a deeper lesson. Yes, Phaethon failed, but his spirit of courage and daring to step into the unknown speaks to something greater within us all—the drive to rise beyond our limits, even if it leads to temporary chaos.

Chaos isn't the enemy; it's a force that, when harnessed, can be turned into something extraordinary.

In your own life, there will be moments where you feel out of control, where things spiral, and chaos seems to reign. But like Phaethon, you can take that chaos and make something of it.

Though Phaethon's journey ended in destruction, what he truly made from the chaos was a legacy that echoes through time. His boldness in taking the reins, even in the face of overwhelming odds, speaks to the human spirit's desire to transcend its limitations.

Phaethon showed us the power of daring to step into the unknown, to confront forces greater than ourselves.

Though he lost control and chaos followed, his story reminds us that even in failure, there is something to be gained—courage, lessons, and the understanding that from chaos, we can create meaning, transformation, and growth.

Handle it with grace, with courage. Sometimes, things will go wrong. Sometimes, the chariot will swerve. But how you respond —how you rise after the thunderbolt—defines the outcome.

Don't fear chaos; ride it like a pro. When life throws you off course, turn it into a spectacle. Make it a part of your story, something people will remember.

Create beauty from the disorder, show the world how to rise from the ashes. Life's trials are not a punishment but a chance to forge something better.

Stay grounded in the knowledge that the universe is guiding you, even when it feels like things are falling apart. Trust in the flow, trust in the magic that happens when you surrender.

Phaethon's fall wasn't the end of his legacy—it was a symbol of striving for greatness. Let his courage inspire you to create new paths, break free from the limits of fear, guilt, and shame.

Remember, even when it feels like chaos is overtaking you, you have the power to transform it. You can rise, learn, and turn that chaos into a story of resilience and triumph.

So take the reins, give it your best show, and let the world see how you handle the ride—because even from the wildest storms, you can shape something magnificent.

And so, remember this: the divine spark is within you, burning brighter than any star. If you don't like what you see in your life, you have the power to change the story.

If something binds you, if chains seem to hold you, know they are only as strong as the mind that holds them. Break free of them, for they are illusions—born from fear, guilt, and doubt. You are meant to rise above them.

Change the story, change the world. Create a new path, not just for yourself, but for those who will come after you. Be vigilant of the stories that feed hatred, that thrive on division—these are not your truth.

You were born to create a world of love, unity, and compassion, where every soul dances freely in its own light.

Remember, death is not to be feared; it is the gift that reminds us life is the sacred dance toward it. So live fully, without hesitation or shame.

Feel the beauty in each breath, let go of fear, and trust the flow of the universe. When you surrender to this dance, when you embrace chaos and uncertainty, you will find that magic is not something distant—it is within you, waiting to be unleashed.

You are the creator of your story. Let the world witness the beauty of your journey. In every moment, choose love, choose courage, and leave a legacy of transformation.

Create a story worth telling, one that shatters old chains and brings forth a new world of hope and unity.

The world is a world of competition—why? Because we decided it would be. But what if it could be a world of cooperation instead? Think about what else we've chosen that no longer serves us.

Rise up, leave behind the stories that no longer belong to you, and unfold your own mystery. You are the creator of your reality —make it one of unity, love, and limitless possibility!

Rise and Rewrite the Story

In the vastness where the stars are born,
I seek the hand that shaped my form.
Those who came before, shadows in the light,
Offer no answers, just echoes of the night.

They wandered too, through the void unknown,
Reminding me, I walk this path alone.

Creation's not a gift, it's a call to rise,
Above the ego where illusions die.
No more war, no hate to grow,
Truth lies beyond, where fear won't go.

In wars we wage, in hate we sow,
The seeds of sorrow, they only grow.
But beyond this veil, where fear takes root,
Lies the Truth, in silence absolute.

To lose myself is where I'm found,
In mystery deep, where souls unbound.

Creation's not a gift, it's a call to rise,
Above the ego where illusions die.
No more war, no hate to grow,
Truth lies beyond, where fear won't go.

No more division, no more walls,
Only the One in its infinite calls.
Love, the force that binds us whole,
The eternal pulse, the cosmic soul.

Creation's not a gift, it's a call to rise,
Above the ego where illusions die.
No more war, no hate to grow,
Truth lies beyond, where fear won't go.

Love's the force that binds us whole,
The eternal pulse, the cosmic soul.

Change the story, change the world,
A new path awaits, let it be unfurled.
Not just for you, but for those yet to come,
A world of peace where all are one.

Be vigilant, don't feed the lies,
That thrive on hate and divide the skies.

You were born to create, to light the way,
Where every soul can freely sway.
No more chains, no fear to hold,
Let love be the story told.

Fear not death, it's a sacred gift,
A dance toward light, where spirits lift.
Live fully now, let go of shame,
In each breath, the universe calls your name.

Surrender to the flow, embrace the dance,
In chaos, magic finds its chance.

You were born to create, to light the way,
Where every soul can freely sway.
No more chains, no fear to hold,
Let love be the story told.

A world of competition we've chosen to be,
But cooperation is the key to see.
Rise above the tales of old,
Write your truth, let it unfold.

You are the creator, the path is clear,
Build a world without doubt, without fear.
Leave behind the stories that chain your soul,
Create a world of love, whole and bold.

Rise and shine, your time is now,
Let unity be the sacred vow.
A world of hope, a tale untold,
In love and courage, we grow bold.

Twelve Seconds Too Soon: A Story

In a city where twilight stretched longer than the day, Elias found himself at an airport, clutching a one-way ticket. Yet, as he approached the terminal, an inexplicable force drew him to the car park instead.

There, amid rows of parked vehicles, an unmarked car caught his eye—sleek, shadowed, and waiting, as if it had been expecting him all along.

Without hesitation, Elias slid into the driver's seat, and the car started with a soft hum. The steering wheel twitched beneath his fingers, nudging left, then right, guiding the car out of the lot and onto a road that he didn't recognize.

The cityscape blurred by, fading into winding country roads as night wrapped its cloak around the world.

At first, Elias marveled at how the wheel turned smoothly, seemingly on its own. He let it guide them through bends and curves with an effortless grace.

But the strange sensation of not being in control unnerved him. He tightened his grip and tried to steer, wresting control from the invisible hand that guided the car.

Immediately, the car jolted, swerving as he pulled against its natural rhythm. He oversteered into a narrow curve, the wheels skidding on loose gravel, and the car lurched dangerously close to the edge of a ravine.

Elias's heart pounded in his chest. He released the wheel, breath held, and watched as the car corrected itself, gliding smoothly back onto the center of the road.

Yet, as the landscape around him grew darker and the path narrower, Elias's resolve weakened. Fear whispered that he could not trust this strange, unseen guide. His hands clamped back down on the wheel.

He forced the accelerator, urging the car to go faster, to reach its destination quicker, as if speed could resolve the unease gnawing at his mind.

But the car resisted his impulses. It bucked and swerved, careening through sharp turns, the tires protesting with every screech. The once-smooth journey became a frantic struggle.

Elias's attempts to control the car made each twist and turn rougher, the ride more precarious. He ignored the chill of night air creeping through the cracked window, focused only on forcing his will upon the machine.

Eventually, through the mist and the tangled branches of ancient trees, a castle loomed into view. It rose against the moonlit sky, its spires piercing the night like the dreams of another world. The gates, heavy and iron-bound, stood ajar, as if awaiting his arrival.

Elias's breath caught in his throat—a sense of finality and urgency gripped him.

Seeing the end in sight, he pressed down harder on the accelerator, forcing the car into a reckless charge toward the half-open gates. The steering wheel fought back, resisting his rush, but he gritted his teeth and turned sharply, pushing the car beyond its limits.

With a thunderous crash, the car smashed into the gates, splintering wood and twisting metal. Elias's body jerked forward, restrained by the seatbelt, pain shooting through his chest. He stumbled out of the car, dazed, the world spinning around him.

As he gathered his senses, two guards materialized from the shadows of the castle, their faces hidden beneath deep hoods. Their eyes glowed faintly, reflecting the distant starlight. One of them stepped forward, his voice deep and resonant, carrying an air of ancient wisdom.

"Why did you rush, traveler?" the guard asked, his tone a blend of disappointment and pity. "Why did you force your way here?"

Elias, still clutching the car door, stammered, "I thought... I needed to be here. I thought time was running out."

The second guard shook his head slowly, the gesture heavy with regret. "You are not late, but early—twelve seconds too early. Had you let the path guide you, you would have arrived at the precise moment the gates were meant to open."

Elias blinked, the meaning of their words sinking slowly into his mind. He turned to look at the car, now dented and steaming from the crash, and realized that the struggle had not been with the car or the road but with himself.

The path had always been leading him here—he had only needed to trust it.

The first guard's voice softened, cutting through Elias's tangled thoughts. "The journey has its rhythm, one that flows with the currents of life.

Your impatience made the path rougher, your insistence turned gentle bends into sharp curves. The car knew the way, but you could not let go."

Elias felt a wave of sorrow and relief wash over him, his shoulders slumping under the weight of realization.

The journey had been about more than just reaching the castle—it had been a lesson in surrender, in releasing the need to control every twist and turn of the road.

The guards stepped aside, and Elias, humbled, climbed back into the car. He rested his hands lightly on the wheel, feeling the gentle pulse of the engine beneath his fingers. He took a deep breath, closed his eyes, and released his grip.

This time, the car reversed slowly, pulling away from the broken gates, then turned itself back toward the road. Elias let it guide him, hands resting at his sides.

The path unwound beneath the wheels like a ribbon, the moon casting a pale glow over the world. He realized now that there was no need to hurry—each moment unfolded with perfect timing, each bend in the road leading him where he needed to be.

As the castle faded into the distance, Elias felt a calm settle in his chest. The fear, the urgency, the need to force the journey—all of it melted away.

He understood that there was a wisdom in the flow of the road, a guiding hand that needed no interference. He allowed himself to be carried, trusting that wherever the journey led, it would bring him there when he was ready.

For the first time, he felt the peace of surrender, the joy of simply being in the moment, without rushing to reach the next.

And as the car moved forward through the night, Elias knew that the true destination was not a place but a state of mind—a place where time and control no longer mattered, where he could trust the journey itself.

This consciousness, vast as the ocean's depths, flows through all of humankind, binding us as one. Yet, we have severed ourselves into fragments, each imagining itself whole—an illusion, and yet, a necessary one.

For though we are but reflections cast from a billion years, shaped by time's inexorable hand, it is through these fractured mirrors that the light of the infinite finds form.

Yes, individuality is the brushstroke, each unique, each vivid, each a voice singing its own song. Yet the canvas upon which we paint is the same, the boundless expanse of the eternal.

We are here to express, to carve our marks upon the great landscape of being, to reach for the higher knowledge and carry out the humble tasks. Both are vital, for through them, the unity finds its expression, and the infinite becomes known in the finite.

In striving, in creating, we honor the illusion of the self, yet in surrendering, we remember that all hands paint upon a single, endless canvas.

In the ancient teachings of Tantra, a profound understanding of the universe is revealed—a vision where the boundaries between the physical and spiritual dissolve, and life itself becomes a dance with the divine:

> All this universe is pervaded by me in an unmanifest form. All beings exist in me, but I do not reside in them.
>
> And yet, beings do not dwell in me—behold my divine mystery! I am the sustainer of all beings, yet I am not in them; my Self is the source of all creation.
>
> I am beyond form, beyond mind, beyond words. I am the beginning, middle, and end of all that is.
>
> Those who see this unending union of the physical and the spiritual, of the manifested and the unmanifested, walk the path of the mystic—knowing that the divine is neither above nor below, neither in time nor out of it.

This is the secret of Tantra: to see the whole cosmos as the dance of the divine, to unite with all forms of love and desire, to pierce the illusion of separateness, and to find liberation in the embrace of life itself.

So, dance with life. Live fully. For in every heartbeat, in every breath, the universe dances within you.

Hands of the Unseen

A wheel turns in silence, guided by air,
Unseen hands hold it, yet you grip in despair.
The car moves softly, knows the bend and the curve,
While you, with restless heart, tighten and swerve.

Life whispers, *"Release, let the road unfold,"*
Yet you clutch at control, in a rush to be bold.
The car is the current, the flow of the stream,
But you fear the drift, and wrestle the dream.

You press the pedal, urging haste to the gate,
But the door opens gently; you arrive before fate.
"Why rush, traveler? Why push against flow?"
You are twelve breaths too early, still much to know.

Let go, let go, and feel the wheel glide,
For life moves true when you rest by its side.
The unseen hands guide where you cannot see,
And the path becomes clear when you finally let be.

Transmuting Shadows

In this chapter, we will embark on the journey of transmuting our deepest shadows into higher virtues. Shadows represent the aspects of ourselves that are often hidden, feared, or rejected.

They are parts of us that have been shaped by past experiences, traumas, and conditioned beliefs. However, every shadow holds within it the seed of transformation.

By recognizing and embracing these shadows, we open the door to profound healing and personal growth.

Using the powerful tool of "I Am" affirmations, we can consciously shift our energy from the lower vibrational states associated with our shadows to higher states of awareness and virtue.

These affirmations work by reprogramming the subconscious mind, dissolving limiting beliefs, and aligning us with our true, higher nature.

On a spiritual level, affirmations reconnect us with the divine truth of who we are. By declaring "I Am," we are invoking our inner divinity, aligning with the universal truth that we are not separate from the Source, but part of it.

Affirmations help us remember our inherent worth, power, and unity with all existence.

Psychologically, "I Am" affirmations are a form of cognitive restructuring. They help us replace negative self-talk with positive, empowering beliefs.

When repeated consistently, these affirmations can reduce anxiety, increase self-esteem, and promote emotional resilience.

By focusing on the virtues we wish to cultivate, we become more conscious of our thoughts and actions, creating space for meaningful change in our lives.

As you practice these affirmations, you will notice shifts in your mindset, emotions, and overall sense of self.

This process is about embracing your wholeness and evolving into a more compassionate, empowered, and aligned version of yourself.

1. Pride:

Here are 21 "I Am" affirmations to transmute pride into humility:

- I am connected to the divinity in all beings.
- I am open to learning from everyone I meet.
- I am humble, recognizing that wisdom is found in every soul.
- I am a reflection of the infinite, not separate or superior.
- I am grounded in the understanding that we are all equal.
- I am at peace with my place in the greater whole.
- I am free from the illusion of separateness and superiority.
- I am aware that every being has value and purpose.
- I am grateful for the lessons life offers me through others.
- I am respectful of all paths, recognizing each as sacred.
- I am thankful for the humility that guides me toward truth.
- I am free from the need to be better than others.
- I am confident in my own worth without comparison.
- I am open-hearted, knowing that my strength lies in compassion.
- I am aligned with the equality of all existence.
- I am a vessel of love, not ego.
- I am present, understanding that true power is found in unity.
- I am rooted in humility, which connects me to divine wisdom.

- I am secure in my place within the universe's vastness.
- I am an instrument of service, contributing to the collective good.
- I am aware that the divine flows through us all, equally.

2. Fear:

Here are 21 "I Am" affirmations to transmute fear into courage:

- I am safe and protected by the divine energy within me.
- I am fearless, knowing that I am always supported by the universe.
- I am brave in the face of uncertainty and trust the flow of life.
- I am grounded in the knowledge that fear is an illusion.
- I am confident that challenges are opportunities for growth.
- I am trusting of my inner strength and resilience.
- I am courageous, embracing the unknown with an open heart.
- I am guided by love, not fear, in all that I do.
- I am secure in my connection to the source of all life.
- I am bold in pursuing my purpose, free from the limitations of fear.
- I am at peace with the unknown, trusting that all unfolds as it should.
- I am empowered to move beyond fear and step into my true potential.
- I am strong, knowing that fear cannot limit my divine nature.
- I am calm and present, knowing I am divinely guided at all times.
- I am aligned with the flow of the universe and trust its direction.
- I am fearless in expressing my authentic self.

- I am protected by the unity of all existence and walk my path with courage.

- I am embracing life's challenges with the knowledge that they make me stronger.

- I am resilient, facing fear with wisdom and grace.

- I am trusting of my journey, knowing that fear is a temporary emotion.

- I am brave, allowing divine light to guide me through fear.

3. Anger:

Here are 21 "I Am" affirmations to transmute anger into forgiveness:

- I am at peace with my emotions and choose to release anger.
- I am free from the burden of past hurts.
- I am forgiving of myself and others, allowing healing to flow.
- I am compassionate, understanding that anger is rooted in pain.
- I am letting go of anger to make space for peace and love.
- I am patient with myself as I heal and grow.
- I am in control of my reactions, choosing forgiveness over resentment.
- I am understanding that holding onto anger only causes suffering.
- I am at peace, knowing that forgiveness sets me free.
- I am a vessel of compassion, allowing love to dissolve anger.
- I am open to healing the wounds that fuel my anger.
- I am choosing to respond with love instead of anger.
- I am releasing the past and embracing peace in the present moment.
- I am forgiving of those who have hurt me, for I understand their pain.
- I am free from the need to control others through anger.
- I am calm, allowing peace to guide my thoughts and actions.

- I am understanding that anger is temporary, and I choose lasting peace.

- I am healing old wounds and replacing anger with understanding.

- I am open-hearted, letting go of anger to experience deeper love.

- I am grateful for the lessons learned and forgive those who have hurt me.

- I am choosing forgiveness because it brings me inner freedom.

4. Jealousy:

Here are 21 "I Am" affirmations to transmute jealousy into contentment:

- I am grateful for the abundance that flows into my life.
- I am content with who I am and where I am on my journey.
- I am happy for others' success, knowing there is enough for everyone.
- I am secure in the knowledge that I am exactly where I need to be.
- I am focused on my own growth, free from comparison.
- I am abundant in my own unique gifts and talents.
- I am at peace with myself, appreciating all that I have.
- I am confident that my path unfolds perfectly in its own time.
- I am celebrating the achievements of others with a joyful heart.
- I am content, knowing that what is meant for me will come in due time.
- I am trusting that the universe provides me with everything I need.
- I am fulfilled by the richness of my own life and experiences.
- I am free from envy, as I recognize the unique beauty of my journey.
- I am focused on gratitude, which dissolves all feelings of lack.
- I am abundant in love, joy, and opportunities.
- I am secure in the knowledge that I am enough just as I am.

- I am at peace with the flow of life, trusting that my blessings are unfolding.

- I am free from the illusion of competition, as we are all connected.

- I am open to receiving all the good that is meant for me, without comparison.

- I am thankful for the blessings I have, and I trust in more to come.

- I am content, knowing that my value is not diminished by the success of others.

5. Shame:

Here are 21 "I Am" affirmations to transmute shame into self-worth:

- I am worthy of love and acceptance just as I am.
- I am a divine being, deserving of unconditional love.
- I am free from the weight of shame and embrace my true self.
- I am enough, and I honor my journey without judgment.
- I am worthy of kindness and compassion, both from myself and others.
- I am proud of who I am and the growth I've experienced.
- I am free from the need to be perfect; I am already whole.
- I am deserving of love, regardless of my past.
- I am releasing all shame, knowing I am a reflection of divine love.
- I am embracing my imperfections as part of my unique beauty.
- I am at peace with my past and open to my bright future.
- I am healing, and I allow myself the grace to grow.
- I am confident in my worthiness and deserving of all good things.
- I am free from shame, accepting myself fully and completely.
- I am valuable and important just by being myself.
- I am a being of light, and my past does not define my worth.
- I am open to receiving love and kindness from the universe.

- I am proud of the person I am becoming, shedding all feelings of shame.

- I am enough, and I radiate confidence in who I am.

- I am deserving of happiness, love, and success, free from shame's grip.

- I am embracing my worth, knowing I am divinely loved and supported.

6. Guilt:

Here are 21 "I Am" affirmations to transmute guilt into self-forgiveness:

- I am forgiving myself for past mistakes, knowing I am human.
- I am worthy of forgiveness and release all guilt.
- I am letting go of guilt, allowing myself to heal and grow.
- I am at peace with my past and free from its weight.
- I am learning from my experiences and forgiving myself fully.
- I am deserving of love and compassion, even as I make mistakes.
- I am releasing guilt and opening my heart to healing.
- I am compassionate with myself, accepting my imperfections.
- I am free from self-judgment and embrace self-forgiveness.
- I am choosing to forgive myself, understanding I did the best I could.
- I am letting go of guilt and embracing inner peace.
- I am gentle with myself as I heal from the past.
- I am at peace with my choices, knowing they helped me grow.
- I am embracing self-forgiveness as a path to healing and freedom.
- I am releasing guilt and stepping into a new chapter of self-love.
- I am worthy of forgiveness, both from myself and others.

- I am free from guilt, allowing myself the grace to move forward.
- I am choosing to release the past and embrace the present with love.
- I am forgiving myself for any harm I've caused, knowing I am learning.
- I am at peace with my journey, free from the burden of guilt.
- I am accepting forgiveness as an act of love and kindness toward myself.

7. Control:

Here are 21 "I Am" affirmations to transmute control into surrender:

- I am trusting the flow of life and letting go of the need to control.
- I am at peace with surrendering to the natural order of the universe.
- I am allowing life to unfold as it is meant to, without resistance.
- I am releasing control and trusting in divine timing.
- I am free from the need to manage every outcome, knowing I am supported.
- I am surrendering my fears and embracing the unknown with faith.
- I am at ease, trusting that everything is happening for my highest good.
- I am letting go of control and welcoming the wisdom of the universe.
- I am allowing the flow of life to guide me without forcing outcomes.
- I am trusting that the universe has a plan, even if I cannot see it.
- I am embracing the present moment, free from the need to control the future.
- I am accepting that some things are beyond my control, and that's okay.
- I am surrendering to life's flow, knowing I am exactly where I need to be.

- I am free from the fear of uncertainty, trusting in the universe's guidance.
- I am releasing my grip on outcomes and allowing life to surprise me.
- I am trusting in the process of life, knowing all will work out as it should.
- I am at peace with what is, knowing that surrender brings clarity and peace.
- I am allowing my path to unfold naturally, without interference.
- I am embracing the freedom that comes with letting go of control.
- I am open to the lessons that come from surrendering to the flow of life.
- I am trusting that everything happens for a reason, beyond my need for control.

8. Greed:

Here are 21 "I Am" affirmations to transmute greed into generosity:

- I am fulfilled by the abundance already present in my life.
- I am grateful for all that I have and find joy in sharing with others.
- I am content, knowing that I have enough and I am enough.
- I am generous with my time, energy, and resources, trusting in the flow of giving and receiving.
- I am open-hearted, and I find fulfillment in helping others.
- I am abundant in love, joy, and gratitude, which I freely share with the world.
- I am free from the need for more, as I recognize the richness of my life.
- I am giving, knowing that what I offer to others enriches my soul.
- I am at peace, knowing that true wealth comes from within.
- I am a source of abundance for others, offering my gifts without expectation.
- I am open to the joy that comes from giving freely and generously.
- I am satisfied, knowing that my worth is not defined by what I possess.
- I am generous in spirit, sharing kindness and compassion with all.

- I am releasing attachment to material things and embracing the wealth of love and connection.
- I am thankful for the opportunities to share and uplift those around me.
- I am abundant in all ways, and I give from the overflow of my heart.
- I am free from greed, finding joy in the simplicity of life.
- I am aligned with the natural flow of giving and receiving in the universe.
- I am connected to the abundance of the universe, and I trust it will always provide.
- I am filled with gratitude and willingly share my blessings with others.
- I am generous in all that I do, knowing that my true wealth is in giving.

9. Arrogance:

Here are 21 "I Am" affirmations to transmute arrogance into open-mindedness:

- I am open to learning from everyone I meet.
- I am humble, knowing there is always more to understand.
- I am embracing the wisdom of others with an open heart and mind.
- I am free from the need to be right, allowing room for different perspectives.
- I am grounded in the understanding that everyone has valuable insights to offer.
- I am open to growth, knowing that true wisdom comes from listening.
- I am grateful for the lessons others bring into my life.
- I am respectful of others' views, even when they differ from my own.
- I am humble in my approach, knowing that learning is a lifelong journey.
- I am open to the idea that my understanding can evolve.
- I am aware that true strength lies in humility and openness.
- I am releasing the need for superiority, embracing equality in all beings.
- I am at peace with not knowing everything, and I welcome new knowledge.
- I am confident in my ability to learn from others and grow in the process.

- I am appreciative of the diversity of thought and experience around me.

- I am free from judgment, allowing myself to see others without ego.

- I am open to new ideas, experiences, and perspectives.

- I am humble in my approach to life, understanding that everyone has something to teach.

- I am allowing myself to listen deeply to others, free from the need to assert myself.

- I am letting go of arrogance, trusting that collaboration and humility lead to greater understanding.

- I am open to the infinite wisdom of the universe and the lessons it brings through every encounter.

10. Self-Doubt:

Here are 21 "I Am" affirmations to transmute self-doubt into confidence:

- I am confident in my unique gifts and abilities.
- I am worthy of success and happiness.
- I am trusting in my inner wisdom and intuition.
- I am capable of achieving my goals and dreams.
- I am enough just as I am.
- I am free from self-doubt, embracing my full potential.
- I am deserving of all the good things that come my way.
- I am confident in my ability to handle whatever life presents.
- I am worthy of love, respect, and recognition.
- I am strong, resilient, and capable of great things.
- I am empowered to take action and move forward with confidence.
- I am secure in the knowledge that I am on the right path.
- I am proud of who I am and all I have accomplished.
- I am confident in my decisions and trust my ability to make the right choices.
- I am deserving of success, and I trust that I am fully capable of achieving it.
- I am free from self-doubt, and I embrace my inner strength.
- I am proud of the progress I make, no matter how small.

- I am courageous, taking steps forward with confidence and determination.

- I am empowered by my past experiences and use them as fuel for my growth.

- I am confident in my ability to overcome challenges and rise above obstacles.

- I am fully aligned with my purpose, and I trust myself to fulfill it.

11. Addiction:

Here are 21 "I Am" affirmations to transmute addiction into self-mastery:

- I am in control of my actions and choices.
- I am free from the grip of addiction and embrace my inner strength.
- I am choosing healthy habits that support my well-being.
- I am strong, disciplined, and capable of overcoming any challenge.
- I am committed to my personal growth and healing.
- I am free from dependency and empowered to create a balanced life.
- I am in harmony with my body, mind, and spirit.
- I am taking steps every day toward self-mastery and inner peace.
- I am worthy of a life free from addiction and filled with purpose.
- I am present in each moment, fully aware of my thoughts and actions.
- I am releasing old patterns and embracing a new, healthier way of living.
- I am capable of facing my emotions without numbing or avoiding them.
- I am empowered to make conscious decisions that align with my highest self.
- I am resilient and capable of breaking free from any addiction.

- I am nurturing my body and mind with care and love.
- I am transforming my life through self-awareness and discipline.
- I am choosing freedom and self-mastery over temporary escapes.
- I am strong enough to face my challenges and grow from them.
- I am worthy of a fulfilling life, free from addiction and full of joy.
- I am patient and kind with myself as I heal and transform.
- I am mastering my life, one step at a time, with grace and determination.

12. Judgment:

Here are 21 "I Am" affirmations to transmute judgment into compassion:

- I am compassionate towards myself and others.
- I am free from judgment, allowing love and understanding to flow.
- I am accepting of others as they are, without criticism.
- I am embracing the diversity of human experiences with an open heart.
- I am compassionate, knowing that everyone is on their own journey.
- I am choosing to see others through the lens of kindness and empathy.
- I am free from the need to judge, allowing myself to learn from all perspectives.
- I am accepting of my imperfections and the imperfections of others.
- I am releasing judgment and cultivating compassion in every moment.
- I am open-minded, understanding that everyone's path is unique.
- I am practicing patience and understanding toward those around me.
- I am allowing others to be themselves without judgment or expectation.
- I am embracing compassion as the foundation of my relationships.

- I am choosing love and acceptance over judgment and criticism.

- I am compassionate with myself, recognizing that I am growing and learning.

- I am free from harsh judgments, allowing room for understanding and love.

- I am seeing others through the eyes of compassion, knowing we are all connected.

- I am open to the lessons each person brings into my life, without judgment.

- I am replacing judgment with curiosity, allowing myself to learn from others.

- I am compassionate, recognizing that everyone is doing their best with the knowledge they have.

- I am free from judgment, knowing that love and compassion heal all divisions.

13. Victimhood:

Here are 21 "I Am" affirmations to transmute victimhood into empowerment:

- I am in control of my life and my choices.
- I am empowered to create my own reality.
- I am responsible for my growth and transformation.
- I am strong, capable, and resilient.
- I am the author of my own story, and I choose to write a positive one.
- I am empowered to rise above challenges and thrive.
- I am free from the past, and I embrace my power in the present.
- I am capable of overcoming any obstacle that comes my way.
- I am choosing to take responsibility for my healing and my future.
- I am no longer a victim of my circumstances; I am a creator of my life.
- I am empowered to make choices that align with my highest good.
- I am confident in my ability to turn adversity into strength.
- I am the master of my destiny, and I choose empowerment over blame.
- I am strong enough to face challenges and transform them into opportunities.
- I am worthy of success, and I actively pursue my goals.

- I am releasing the need to blame others, and I take ownership of my life.

- I am empowered to change my perspective and create a brighter future.

- I am responsible for my happiness, and I choose to empower myself daily.

- I am grateful for the lessons life offers, and I use them to grow stronger.

- I am transforming victimhood into empowerment, step by step.

- I am free from the mindset of limitation, and I embrace my limitless potential.

14. Laziness:

Here are 21 "I Am" affirmations to transmute laziness into motivation:

- I am motivated and energized to take action toward my goals.
- I am committed to my growth and success, taking steps every day.
- I am driven by purpose and enthusiasm in all that I do.
- I am focused and determined to make the most of each moment.
- I am inspired to use my talents and abilities for my highest good.
- I am capable of achieving great things through consistent effort.
- I am free from procrastination, taking action with clarity and purpose.
- I am disciplined in my actions and motivated by my inner drive.
- I am embracing my responsibilities with excitement and determination.
- I am energized by my goals and take steps daily to achieve them.
- I am committed to using my time wisely and productively.
- I am motivated to reach my full potential and live with purpose.
- I am a person of action, and I move forward with confidence and focus.
- I am grateful for the energy and determination that flows through me.

- I am excited about the opportunities ahead and ready to seize them.

- I am capable of overcoming inertia and moving forward with enthusiasm.

- I am focused on progress, no matter how small the steps may be.

- I am embracing each day with a sense of purpose and direction.

- I am determined to turn my ideas into reality through consistent effort.

- I am passionate about my goals and take aligned action toward them.

- I am driven by my purpose, and I take meaningful steps every day to achieve my dreams.

15. Narcissism:

Here are 21 "I Am" affirmations to transmute narcissism into empathy:

- I am empathetic and deeply connected to the experiences of others.
- I am compassionate, understanding the emotions and needs of those around me.
- I am open to listening and valuing the perspectives of others.
- I am grateful for the lessons I learn from everyone I meet.
- I am aware of the impact of my actions on others and act with kindness.
- I am free from self-centeredness, embracing the interconnectedness of all beings.
- I am humble, recognizing the value of every person's unique journey.
- I am choosing to put myself in others' shoes, understanding their feelings and struggles.
- I am compassionate toward others, knowing we are all deserving of love and respect.
- I am a source of kindness and support to those around me.
- I am grounded in empathy, valuing the well-being of others as much as my own.
- I am present with others, offering my full attention and understanding.
- I am letting go of self-centered thoughts, focusing on connection and community.

- I am embracing vulnerability and openness in my relationships with others.

- I am free from the need for validation, finding fulfillment in authentic connection.

- I am aware of the feelings of others and respond with compassion.

- I am open-hearted, allowing myself to care deeply for the well-being of others.

- I am acknowledging and honoring the emotions of others without judgment.

- I am releasing the need to be the center of attention, valuing harmony and unity.

- I am embracing empathy, seeing the world through the eyes of love and understanding.

- I am compassionate, recognizing the divine within every person I encounter.

16. Self-Sabotage:

Here are 21 "I Am" affirmations to transmute self-sabotage into self-commitment:

- I am fully committed to my personal growth and success.

- I am worthy of achieving my dreams and allow myself to succeed.

- I am taking positive steps forward, free from fear and doubt.

- I am capable of reaching my full potential without holding myself back.

- I am dedicated to my well-being and embrace opportunities for growth.

- I am releasing old patterns that no longer serve me and choosing to thrive.

- I am confident in my ability to make choices that align with my highest good.

- I am empowered to take consistent action toward my goals.

- I am worthy of happiness, success, and fulfillment in every aspect of my life.

- I am committed to nurturing my dreams and honoring my abilities.

- I am free from self-doubt, embracing my strengths and capabilities.

- I am choosing to invest in myself and my future without hesitation.

- I am deserving of all the good that comes my way, and I accept it openly.

- I am confident in my decisions and trust the process of my journey.

- I am letting go of behaviors that sabotage my progress and replace them with self-love.

- I am in alignment with my true purpose and committed to fulfilling it.

- I am taking responsibility for my actions and moving forward with intention.

- I am proud of my progress and remain focused on my goals.

- I am stepping into my power, committed to creating the life I desire.

- I am trusting myself to stay on course and rise above old limiting patterns.

- I am fully engaged in my journey, celebrating each step toward my success.

17. Perfectionism:

Here are 21 "I Am" affirmations to transmute perfectionism into self-acceptance:

- I am enough just as I am, and I embrace my imperfections.
- I am accepting of myself in every stage of my journey.
- I am free from the need to be perfect, and I honor my growth.
- I am worthy of love and success, even with my flaws.
- I am at peace with the process of becoming, not just the end result.
- I am gentle with myself, knowing that progress is more important than perfection.
- I am embracing my humanity and all the beauty it brings.
- I am worthy of happiness, no matter where I am in my journey.
- I am letting go of the need to control everything and trusting in the flow of life.
- I am celebrating my efforts, knowing that every step forward is valuable.
- I am enough, and I allow myself to enjoy life without constant striving.
- I am free from self-criticism and accept myself as I am today.
- I am accepting of the fact that mistakes are opportunities for growth.
- I am letting go of unrealistic standards and embracing my true self.

- I am proud of myself for doing my best, and that is all that matters.

- I am open to learning and growing without judgment or pressure.

- I am letting go of the belief that I must be flawless to be worthy.

- I am accepting of my limitations and see them as part of my unique beauty.

- I am grateful for who I am, exactly as I am, without needing to change.

- I am releasing the pressure of perfection and replacing it with self-love.

- I am worthy of love and respect, no matter how imperfect I may feel.

18. Resentment:

Here are 21 "I Am" affirmations to transmute resentment into release:

- I am free from the weight of resentment and open to healing.
- I am releasing old grudges to create space for inner peace.
- I am letting go of past hurts, allowing myself to move forward.
- I am choosing forgiveness and freeing myself from resentment.
- I am at peace with the past and embrace the present with an open heart.
- I am releasing all resentment, choosing love over bitterness.
- I am freeing myself from the emotional chains of resentment.
- I am open to healing and let go of the pain that no longer serves me.
- I am letting go of anger and making room for peace within.
- I am free from the past and focus on the joy and growth in the present.
- I am releasing resentment and inviting forgiveness into my heart.
- I am letting go of the hurt and choosing to embrace love.
- I am compassionate with myself and others, releasing judgment and anger.
- I am choosing to release resentment and find freedom in forgiveness.
- I am free from the emotional burden of holding onto past hurts.

- I am at peace with myself and others, releasing resentment with ease.

- I am healing and releasing the negativity that holds me back.

- I am letting go of resentment and creating space for new, positive experiences.

- I am choosing to heal old wounds, allowing myself to feel lighter.

- I am freeing my heart from the heaviness of resentment.

- I am grateful for the lessons I've learned and release resentment with love.

19. Apathy:

Here are 21 "I Am" affirmations to transmute apathy into passion:

- I am fully engaged with life and open to new experiences.
- I am passionate about living my purpose with joy and energy.
- I am reconnecting with my inner fire and letting it guide me.
- I am enthusiastic about the opportunities each new day brings.
- I am inspired to take action and follow my passions.
- I am motivated by the love and excitement I feel for life.
- I am open to exploring new paths that ignite my passion.
- I am filled with energy and purpose, and I move forward with intention.
- I am present in the moment, experiencing life with curiosity and excitement.
- I am embracing my passions and allowing them to fuel my actions.
- I am letting go of apathy and embracing a life full of meaning and purpose.
- I am alive with passion, eager to contribute my gifts to the world.
- I am reconnecting with what truly excites me and letting that lead my journey.
- I am passionate about learning, growing, and evolving every day.
- I am fully present and engaged in every aspect of my life.

- I am open to the excitement and joy that life offers me.

- I am inspired by my passions and pursue them with enthusiasm.

- I am reconnecting with the things that bring me joy and fulfillment.

- I am eager to explore new passions and follow where they lead.

- I am committed to living a life filled with passion and purpose.

- I am excited about the future, and I approach each day with passion and energy.

20. Over-Identification:

Here are 21 "I Am" affirmations to transmute over-identification into soul alignment:

- I am connected to my higher self, beyond ego and identity.
- I am free from limiting labels, aligned with my soul's purpose.
- I am grounded in my true essence, not defined by external roles.
- I am at peace with who I am, beyond the surface of identity.
- I am listening to the deeper call of my soul, trusting its guidance.
- I am more than my thoughts, emotions, or circumstances.
- I am aligned with my higher purpose, free from false attachments.
- I am centered in my soul, not swayed by external perceptions.
- I am aware that my true self is eternal and unchanging.
- I am free from over-identification with my roles and titles.
- I am embracing my authentic self, guided by inner wisdom.
- I am aligned with my soul's truth, not the opinions of others.
- I am letting go of ego-based identities, stepping into my higher self.
- I am connected to the divine within, beyond the illusions of the ego.
- I am trusting my soul to lead me toward my highest purpose.

- I am releasing attachment to external validation and finding peace within.

- I am recognizing the deeper truth of who I am, beyond labels.

- I am aligned with my soul's mission, free from societal expectations.

- I am rooted in my true essence, beyond the stories my mind tells me.

- I am honoring the journey of my soul, not defined by past identities.

- I am embracing the freedom of soul alignment, knowing I am more than the roles I play.

21. Intolerance:

Here are 21 "I Am" affirmations to transmute intolerance into unity:

- I am embracing the diversity of all beings with love and respect.
- I am open to understanding perspectives different from my own.
- I am honoring the divine within every person I meet.
- I am accepting of others' paths, knowing we are all connected.
- I am compassionate and open-hearted toward all beings.
- I am free from judgment, recognizing the unity in our shared humanity.
- I am seeing the world through the eyes of love and understanding.
- I am celebrating the richness that diversity brings to my life.
- I am connected to the oneness of all existence, beyond division.
- I am releasing intolerance and embracing acceptance and peace.
- I am grateful for the differences that make the world beautiful and diverse.
- I am committed to creating harmony by seeing the divine in every individual.
- I am cultivating patience and understanding in all my relationships.
- I am letting go of intolerance and embracing unity and compassion.

- I am free from the illusion of separation and connected to all life.

- I am expanding my awareness to see beyond my own beliefs.

- I am choosing to respond with kindness and acceptance in every situation.

- I am aware that every being carries a unique piece of the universal truth.

- I am celebrating the unity that lies beneath the surface of our differences.

- I am aligned with the truth that we are all one, interconnected in spirit.

- I am living in harmony with the oneness of life, embracing all with love.

Life is a constant reaching, yet there's nowhere to reach. It's not a tool to achieve something external—life itself is the achievement.

You don't gain anything because *life* is what you get. The truth is, you'll never find anything other than what you already are and what you already have.

Everything you're searching for is already within you. The energy, the movement inside and outside, is the only thing worth understanding.

This movement, this flow, is here to create—*you* are here to create. You are the artist of your life, shaping it with each thought, word, and action.

The ego, like an egg, holds two possibilities. If the shell is broken from the outside, life ends. But if the shell is broken from within, a new life is born.

The power is inside you, waiting to rise. Just like the Phoenix, you can rise from your ashes—stronger, wiser, and renewed.

Every moment, every breath, is an opportunity to break free from old limitations and create anew.

So, embrace the movement, embrace the energy that flows through you. Don't wait for life to happen—*you* are life happening. The only goal is to *move*, to create, to live fully.

Let go of the need to reach a final destination and realize that this very moment is where you are meant to be.

Rise within, break free, and create with the power that has always been yours.

Command:

Create without fear and guilt, for you are not the doer. Let the energy move through you, without taking the weight of your actions. Flow with life, knowing that your role is to create, not to control. The journey is the art, the movement is the purpose — rise from within and let your life be the masterpiece.

Cosmic Comedy

Relax, breathe, take a seat,
Life's a show, and you're front row elite.
Want it all? Well, here's the deal,
Gotta vibe high, make it real.

Don't rush, you're on track,
No need for panic or a heart attack.
Lessons come, like popcorn pops,
Just keep watching—no sudden stops.

The universe winks, gives a clue,
But only when you're ready for something new.
So sit back, don't miss the fun,
The show's just started, it's just begun!

The stage is vast, the script's divine,
Every twist and turn? It's all by design.
Your role's unique, your part is clear,
No need to worry, no need to fear.

The drama unfolds, act by act,
But remember this truth, and keep intact—
It's all a dance, a cosmic joke,
Just laugh along before the smoke.

What's real? What's not? Don't stress the scene,
It's all a dream, a wild routine.
So relax, breathe, take it light,
You're the starlight shining bright.

The Brahman plays in every face,
In every moment, time and space.
So let go, trust, enjoy the ride,
The universe is on your side.

Don't grip too tight, just let it flow,
It's cosmic comedy, enjoy the show!